Close to the Ground

Ground

A collection of poems
by Nancy Thomas
2016

BARCLAY PRESS
Newberg, OR 97132

Close to the Ground

A Collection of Poems
by Nancy Thomas

Published by Barclay Press
Newberg, Oregon

www.barclaypress.com
www.barclaypress.com/nancythomas

ISBN 978-1-59498-036-7

COVER PHOTOGRAPH: Donovan Aylard

Dedicated to
the next generation of
poets, sculptors, musicians,
painters, chain-saw carvers,
dancers and story-tellers,
chief among whom are
Bree and Jade Becker,
Thomas Reilly Gault,
Aren Daniel Thomas,
Gwen Emily Amahoro Thomas,
Paige Rebecca Gault,
Alandra Uwizera Thomas, and
Peter Morgan Gault.

Contents

Prologue

Ordinary grace disguises itself in faded irises, traffic signs, convoluted "meetings for worship for business," and the funny things small children say. Many years ago I discovered my vocation as a poet who sees and expresses the grace of God hidden in the ordinariness of life. This grace hovers close to the ground.

The first section, "Playing with Words," celebrates language itself. C. S. Lewis wrote, "The serious business of heaven is joy." I underlined that passage and later adapted it to my vocation: "The serious business of the poet is play." What we poets play with so seriously are words. We catch them in butterfly nets, juggle them, toss them high, and read the ground where they land. We acknowledge that language changes, and while we may be indignant at how some people manhandle words, we can laugh at the results.

I have entitled the second section, "Family Scrapbook." It celebrates memory, one of the ancient traditions of the Christian faith. My memories are specific—small incidents from the past, word altars that recall faces, messages, and relationships that take on life again in the remembering. From my decision that I was too old to kiss my parents goodnight, to my first trophy won for a speech on world peace, a roller coaster ride to celebrate my fiftieth birthday, and a conversation with a sunshine-eating granddaughter, I am constantly reminded of grace.

The third section, "The Absurdity of Prayer," focuses on

the human side of our relationship with God. It notices the klutziness of being the church. It celebrates a spirituality with dirt on its face and saints with sullied reputations. Several of the poems draw their inspiration from the Scriptures, and while the commentary may be unorthodox, I make it with respect. Whatever critique these poems contain is laced with affection.

The final section, "Longing for Home," affirms the hope of resurrection and new life. "Like Moses, I approach the thick darkness where God is—groping, breathless, ready." On all the weary roads that have led to today, I recognize that angels were singing.

Grace was—is—ever present. And all things, those in the heavens and those closer to the ground, are from, through, and to God. Glory.

1
Playing with Words
The serious business of the poet is play.

Morning Watch

William Stafford, that kind poet,
once told me how he got up
at 4:00 every morning
to sit in the quiet and wait for a poem.
It always came. Stafford filled notebooks
with the fruit of his attention and freely
shared it with the world. I'm grateful
to have been included in that world.
So here am I, sitting in my own
quiet spot by a window. The morning
grows light before me. Trees emerge
and the far hills. Like Stafford,
I'm waiting. Waiting.

Mother Tongue

She was there in the beginning. She licked my face
as I gathered spindly legs and lurched to my feet.
She nurtured me through the pastures of childhood,
under youth's dark skies and into the dawning
of this day. A generous but imperfect gift,
an uneven mix of many family lines,
she gave me no smooth pedigree, but rather
the keys to a mysterious kingdom. As she
told me the stories, I learned to graze
on the words, to swallow them little
by little, to let them settle, digest.
They became part of my flesh, are today
part of my fleshing out as I move through spheres
of sound and silence, namer and poet,
participant in the world of all things.

Nairobi Speaks

(From signs on the backs of vehicles
in a traffic jam, Nairobi, 2008)

"Belt up please."
The Department of Motor Vehicles thanks you.
The chief of police thanks you.
The entire municipality of greater Nairobi
is obligated to you for your compliance
with our regard
for your personal safety.

****

"Instant brakes!"
Just add water
as in torrents of rain,
with a riot or two,
a traffic jam and the clash
of cultures thrown in,
and, *voilá!*
See me stop!

****

"Throwing out trash is highly prohibited."
This is no mere suggestion.
A solemn recommendation
of profound import
urges you to clutch your candy
wrapper and keep the windows
up. Don't even imagine letting it float
out. We really mean it.

I Give My Word

"Do you give me your word?"
he asked at the end of our Serious Talk.
My word? I wondered. Do I own a word,
and which one would it be?
And how would I give it away?

I have many favorite words.
Some are small and simple,
like *stone* or *salt* or *sea*.
Would he want one of those?
Some are long and funny,
even when they frown,
like *preposterous* or *obstreperous*,
ludicrous or *lugubrious*.
"Here," I could say.
"Have some *preposterous*."
Would that one satisfy his need?

I imagine reaching deep
into my word bag and randomly
pulling out *poodle* or *possum*, *amber*

or *ambiguity, sizzle, syrup*
or that old stand-by, *stuff*.
And it's true that if these lovely
pebbles are mine in any sense,
they're only mine to give away,
whether polished or crude.

So here's what I choose.
I will give him *grace*.

Then all the rest
are his for the having.

The Lurch

He went and left me in the lurch,
but I don't mind much because
it's a very nice lurch.
It reminds me of a yurt,
only not so round on top.
It's yellow with fleece rugs.
There are no windows but he
supplied it with some
of my favorite foods like passion-
fruit and beef jerk-
y and a whole bag of blue
M&Ms so I'll do just fine,
thank you. I wish he
hadn't gone, actually,
but at least I have
the satisfaction of knowing
that he left me in the lurch.

"A Good Time Was Had by All"

(Line from the local newspaper report of a social event)

The grocer proposed a toast and affirmed that
    without a doubt a Good Time was being had by him.
The high school football coach, speaking for the
    whole team, barked that It was being had by all of them,
    too.
The local beauty queen's hot pink smile and
    fluttering luscious lashes gave ample
    testimony that It had not passed her by.
The protestant pastor winked and said that not
    only a Good Time but a genuine God Time
    had been had by him and his grateful flock.
The local politician smiled directly at the
    camera, then proclaimed, "The Good Time
    has not only been had, It's been sponsored
    by me at no cost to the general public."
At long last the aforementioned General Public,
    in holiday uniformity, also fully admitted to
    having had It.
So everyone went home.

"God's Tiny Hand"
The Bolivian Soccer Team Asks a Blessing

(From the headline of the sports section of El Deber, March 26, 2005, the day before Easter: "Una Manito de Dios")

Our Father Which Art
in Heaven, on earth, and most especially in Bolivia,
hallowed and hollered be your name.
We, who bow to no one,
bend our heads in devotion to seek your blessing
this Holy Week. We remember
your death, and plead that it not be in vain,
plead that you remember our Life and let
us win tomorrow's game.
Resurrect our hopes to place.
Let next year's Cup not pass from us.
Bless our kicks, our passes, our
blocks and our sprints. Let us score
against the enemy, whose name is
Argentina. Reward our faith.
Grant peace to our land and goals to our team.
Give us just a tiny helping Hand,
and we will inscribe your name
forever in our hearts
and on our trophies.
Amen.

Toast

"If you don't"—don't what? I forget
that part—"you're toast," he told me.
What he doesn't know is that I'm
already toast. I've been toast all
my life. Consider the evidence:
    -I'm a morning person.
    -I like wearing black—the color
        of burnt toast,
      -burnt because I often hesitate
        before manifesting
    -although I have also been known
        to pop up prematurely.
    -The crumbs on my face—
      what do they say?
I will offer this in my favor—
    the crunch I make
    is a pleasing sound.

On Being Good

1. Brief Conversation in the Foyer of the Church

How ya doin today, Nancy? Ya good?

> *Well, I'm not evil. As far as*
> *goodness goes, I'm inching*
> *forward, but not quite there*
> *yet. What about yourself?*

OK....Ya know, I don't really have time
for this right now.

> *Good isn't about time and doing.*
> *It's about essence. Being.*
> *It inhabits time without being enslaved*
> *to time. It goes with you, sort of*
> *like your skin.*

Whatever. Catch ya later.

> *Later.*

2. Short Conversation with God

> *Good morning, Lord.*
> *How are you today? Ya good?*

> Yep. I'm good.

"Don't Play with Your Food"

Now that I'm grown up,
out from under their rules,
I can do it all I want.
And I do. I grab the carrot
sticks and rat-a-tat-tat
on my water glass; a cool
rhythm accompanies my meal.
Peas are a little small for juggling
but it's satisfying to see how high
they go, feel them rain back,
catch a few in my mouth.
Dinner goes well
in the old doll house. In front
of the potato couch, I squirt
a Ketchup carpet, then scatter random
pickle slices as area rugs. Radishes
make nifty stools, and a hollowed
out dinner roll becomes a bathtub
to die for, should I ever wish to die
in my bath. Mealtimes
have become more pleasant

than I could have dreamed of
as a child. I laugh a lot.
No one yells.

On Oxymorons

My friend can't decide
whether his creative process
is logically intuitive
or intuitively logical.
"Why not both?" I say.
One lone oxymoron
is simply a stupid cow.
But with a matched pair,
then, O then!
you can plow a field.

For Your Information

I'm going to be famous someday—
a great poet
    textbooked
    lauded
    quoted
    analyzed
    and frankly famous.
It's a statistical fact.
If I write 200 poems a year
    20 will be good
    2 will be great.
So—if I live 25 more years
    (a mathematical probability)
    that's 50 great poems.

As soon as I get around to it,
I simply must clear some space
for the trophies.

I Love Tangents

I love them in all colors.
I love the orange ones that shock me
    with their brazen gestures and their teasing.
I love the lavender tangents, and the tangents
    that shift from blue to green; I love
    their innuendos, their hisses, their
    strange and lovely lies.

I love them in all shapes and sizes
    —the small round tangents, deceptively
    easy to handle, but once lost, impossible
    to retrieve;
    —the proper boxed tangents, predictable,
    safe, they serve as hobbies on
    application forms.

I love the scent of tangents
    and how you can always know
    when one's coming by the slight pungency
    humming on the edges of the afternoon.

Once an unusually potent tangent
    let me ride it and we went for miles,
    clear to Montana and back in less time
    than it takes to whistle the "1812 Overture."
    I still haven't recovered.

The Dysfunctional Poet Lays the Blame

It all goes back
to my father. He worried
words, fidgeted the adjectives,
broke down the verbs
until even their etymological
parts were unrecognizable.
He flung participles
against the walls, as I sat
and watched the fragments
fall. "See what you have
to look forward to,
Nancy," he said.

Ready or Not

It's spring
and already poems
are flitting around me
in such numbers I
need a butterfly net
to capture them.
Multiple reds
and greens and blues
and blindingly bright
yellows hum their lively
wings. One alights
on my hand. It levitates
and heads west
before I can properly greet
it. But no matter.
My eyes are open.
My inner net is poised.
I'm ready.

The Poet's Gifts

Praise ambiguity
    —two separate paths
       and no road signs
    —scales that tip
       first one way then the other
    —the enticement of not knowing
    —the scent on the wind
       that beckons me enter the forest

Praise silence
    —the space between the words
    —the secret behind the sound
    —the barely perceptible still-small-voice

Praise indirection
    —the path that winds
       through whispering groves
    —brush that obscures
       whatever lies ahead
    —the gloriously dizzying circles
    —distractions, interruptions and surprises
       everywhere

Praise subtlety
 —the minuscule wildflowers
  of an *altiplano* spring
 —secret rainbows on sea shells
  no one finds
 —a discernible dearth of exclamation
  points and adjectives
 —that chuckle in the dark

Praise clarity
 —blue skies and a straight path
 —knowing the names of the trees
 —knowing several reasons why
 —a stark prophetic word

Praise paradox
 —clarity greets her strange cousins,
  ambiguity and indirection
 —they decide to spend the day in the park
 —the cousins play in the sand box
  while clarity tends the community garden
 —later they walk home holding hands
 —they know the place when they get there

Praise simplicity
 —small words like salt, sand, grass, bug
 —homemade bread and truth
 —no need to impress
 —being above doing
 —doing that flows from love

—and after it's done
    sweet sleep

Praise specificity
    —a beetle is better than a bug
    —not city, or worse—urban configuration
        but Cochabamba, Kigali,
        Cincinnati, Istanbul
    —a plant flourishes
        as a nasturtium, sequoia
        or licorice fern
    —walking through the world of all things
        naming them one by one

Praise mystery
    —not yet knowing something, sensing
        its urgency, loving the chase
    —recognition that hide-n-seek
        is holy play
    —hope that all of this is more than game
    —love for the questions
    —faith that the paths lead home

Praise playfulness
    —juggling the words, tossing
        them high, watching them
        catch the sun
    —placing the puzzle pieces
        one by one, letting the picture
        emerge

—it's OK to stomp through mud
   puddles, track a grimy truth
   into the house
—humus, humility and humor
   join human in a circle
   play ring-around-the-rosey
   then fall on the grass laughing
—"Knock, knock."
   "Who's there?"
   "Behold-I-stand-at-the-door. That's who."*
   "Come in! Come in!"
   say the children and the poets.

*Thanks to Julie Peyton for the "knock knock" joke.

2
Family Scrapbook

It's hard to be six.

I'm Sorry

I was 13 when I decided
I was too old to kiss you
goodnight. You didn't protest,
sensing, I suppose, my adolescent
need for separation. I simply
said, "No," you simply
nodded, and that was that.
I never kissed you again.

First Place

At the age of 14, I won my first speech contest.
Before the judges of the Reedley Rotary Club
and a select group of peers, I declaimed on the topic,
"People to People: Key to World Understanding."
My formula for world peace as a high school
freshman should have won first place for audacity,
but I didn't know that. I just blushed
and accepted the trophy. Some twenty years later,
in a fit of simplicity, I threw out my old trophies
and now I sort of regret it. World peace has not yet
been accomplished. Nevertheless, something solid
remains—the image of my dad sitting on my bed,
listening to me practice; bald Mr. Kornelson,
in his usual black suit and red bow tie, standing
at the back of the auditorium, nodding vigorously
at each word even though he had the speech
memorized; Mrs. Glantz reading aloud
the announcement the next day in first period
algebra. She later told me she knew I could
do it. She wasn't even surprised.

Magic Mountain

The last time I rode a roller coaster
I had just turned 50. I'm not sure
what made me get on, but somehow
I found myself belted in, gripping
the arm of my husband of some 25-plus
years, as we started the slow ascent.
Its name, "The Viper," should have
made me think twice. I thought more
than twice on the way up. "I'm
sorry for everything," I prayed, eyes
shut tight. "Please save me." Poised
three seconds at the top, I forgot to breathe.
Breath and prayer became irrelevant
as we plummeted down, then up
and around and down again, trees and
buildings a blur, the death grip
on my loved one's arm tightening.
But somewhere on that last curve,
seconds before we eased to the station,
I looked at him. He looked at me. We grinned.
The third time around I sang Psalms.

Conversation with Hal on Waste Removal

On the way home
from our early morning walk,
Hal pointed to the vacant lot
across the street, drawing
my attention to a Black Thing
resting in the weeds.
He asked, "Is that a crow
or a cat?" "Or a garbage
bag?" I wondered out
loud, adding to the list
of Mysteries. I was half-way
convinced of my own perspective,
when the garbage
bag levitated, twitched
its tail, and casually
ambled off. "Too bad
it really wasn't a garbage
bag," I offered. "You're crazy,"
wasn't spoken out loud,
but he said it nonetheless. "Look
at it this way," I posited.

"What an option this
would give us for waste
removal. Just say to the trash,
'Go there,' and it would arise
and go, without expensive
vehicles or the cost
of personnel. Just think."
He conceded my point
as we, imitating the garbage
bag, ambled on home.

A Reassuring Conversation

"How'd I do?" he asked me on the drive home.
"I know I was prepared, but was I interesting?"

"Yes, I think so," I replied.

"But *how* interesting? Was anyone bored?"

"They seemed to be following you."

"But is that good enough? I read about people who
make scintillating conversation. Do I ever do that?
And what does that mean? Sparkle? Fire? What?" he pressed.

"I'll look it up when we get home," I offered.

"This evening, for example," he continued.
"Did I actually scintillate?"

"Yes, Hal, I think you did," I said, feeling my way.
"But don't worry about it.
Better scintillate than never."

Advice to My Son and His Wife
on Bringing Home Their First Baby

Stop asking me to wash my hands
before picking her up.

No, it's not my turn. You change her.
This is no game; we no longer
take turns.

Yes, it's OK to dress her in a blue sweater,
wrap her in a blue blanket,
give her the blue rabbit
Great-Aunt Millie sent.

Take her outside for a walk
under the filbert trees.
Show her the green ceiling.
Let her feel the breeze.

Keep reading out loud—
The Count of Monte Cristo,
The Lord of the Rings, the book

of Jeremiah, *Winnie-the-Pooh*.
Don't explain anything.
She'll get it.

Don't talk baby talk. Ever.
Discuss great thoughts with her—
destiny, human rights, freedom.
Start now. She's ready.

Don't put her in the church nursery.
Let her sit through the prayers,
the soggy music, the silences.
Something will get through.
(And she may liven things up.)

Teach her "This Little Piggy,"
"The Itsy Bitsy Spider," and
"This Old Man." Pass on your
cultural heritage. It is a treasure,
however buried.

Don't let her eat buttons or mushrooms.
Door knobs are larger and will do
just as well.

Listen very closely
to all she has to teach you.
Start now. You're ready.

The Grandchildren Speak

1. Paige

I was sitting in the easy chair a few evenings ago
when Paige, pajamaed, brushed, and smelling of
   toothpaste,
came over, placed her hands on my knees, put her face
up into mine, and purred, "I won't ever kill
you, 'cause you're my favorite grandma."
Thank God. One less thing to worry about.

2. Reilly

Saturday. Bad day right from the start.
"No! I don't want to get up!"
"No! I don't want to stay in bed!"
"Cheerios? Yuck."
"Mom! Make Paige give that to me! It's my robot!"
A general no to everything.
And then it happened. A gigantic wet sneeze
left him as surprised as the rest of us.
A brief pause, and tears began rolling down his face.
Kristin, Good Mother, reached out.
"Reilly, what's wrong?" "When I sneeze,"

he wailed, "my cheeks get cold
and I don't know how to get them warm again."
Kristin's laugh didn't help.
It's hard to be six.

3. Peter

You didn't talk at all for a long time,
and it warms me that one of your first words
was *light*, and your first sentence, *light on*, as you pointed
to the correct spot on the ceiling or toward the window.
Light has always drawn you, even at four months
when the experts pronounced you blind, told us
there was no cure, and we gathered our courage,
began checking out books on Braille.
But now at two you navigate the shores and shoals
of this house with more than your inner compass. You
    reach
for favorite toys, recognize people before they speak,
and point to pictures in books saying,
"Doggy! Doggy! Woof!" You've been promoted to
visually impaired, but we hold the label lightly.
Clearly the lights are on. Sail forth, young Peter.
Show us the way.

On Giving a Present to a Nine-Year-Old

Not at all prepared, the Big Day
sneaks up and I have to buy
something, anything. So
I settle for a grab bag type
of gift—an assortment
of surprises. Why is it so
important that she like it?
Is this how she measures
my love? At nine years old,
perhaps. So I assemble; first,
a stuffed jack rabbit,
its quirky extended
front feet redeeming it
from the mass of beasts
already littering her room.
And the small glittering
butterfly broach, almost like
real jewelry. Good enough
for her? I hope so. For good
measure I throw in crayons—self-
sharpening—and an artist's tablet

of blank paper, prods to her
imagination. Back at home,
I realize I don't have wrapping
paper, so the plastic bag
announcing "Staples" in bright red
letters will have to do. As I get out
of the car, I fret, "Will she like this?
Is it enough? Can she sense
how special she is to us?" Then
the relief, the silly relief.
"Grandma! Is this for me?!
I love his feet! How soft!
How beautiful! Can I pin it on
now?" Such small things. I continue
to wonder, how does the love
manage to seep through?
Happy birthday, Alandra.

The Sunshine Eater

Bree eats sunshine.
Every sunny morning
at precisely 10:30
she goes outside,
lifts her head to the sky,
opens her mouth
and lets the golden rays
slip down her throat.
They fill her body
with light.
She does it simply
because it's good,
as right as oranges
and generosity,
as regular exercise,
doing your homework early
and helping with the dishes.
And also because it feeds
the butterflies in her stomach.
Such a diet of sun
brings out the brilliant

colors in their wings—the reds
and yellows and deep sea
blues. Otherwise, the butterflies
would turn brown and mushy,
she says. That's exactly
what she says, this bright,
courageous and slightly audacious
sunshine eating girl.

Watching the Hippo Die

We approached the lake slowly,
easing our vehicle over the ruts.
Spotting something at the water's edge,
we wondered if it were a giant hippo
or merely a large grey rock.
We were not the first to stop
or the first to see whatever
it was there in the water. Some distance
away, closer to it than we were, a van
loaded with tourists had parked.
The man standing outside was obviously
a guide. He pointed to the object, shouted
something, then bent down to gather stones.
We watched him throw them, mostly missing
at first. But when one hit the mark,
what was unmistakably a huge hippo
slowly raised his head, then just as slowly
lowered it back into the water.
The guide continued pelting,
getting more accurate with practice.
As one particular stone hit hard,

the animal raised its head higher,
and we saw what appeared to be a large yellow tusk.
Obviously an old beast, it became clear
to us that he was dying. No longer able
to move quickly or to submerge his bulk,
he just lay there in the shallows, finally
refusing to even raise his head. We had to leave,
and when we passed the place again
several hours later, he was still there,
motionless. The only evidence
of the guide and the tourists
were the scattered stones along the shoreline
and the tracks of their van,
long gone.

Why I Want to Own a Platypus

I have this collection of wooden
birds from Bolivia. Parrot,
toucan, woodpecker, hummingbird,
owl, goose, duck, flamingo and a flock
of small, nameless warblers
perch on convenient spaces
around my apartment. All native
to South America, they stir
memories and fill this indoor
air with silent song. On my last
trip to La Paz, I noticed a few
wooden platypuses for sale in the tourist
shops. Of course, I resisted. For one
thing, these beasts are every bit
as much tourists as the folks
who would buy them. Australian,
probably. Definitely not native.
For another thing, they look more
like cartoons than real animals.
And finally, in spite of its weird
birdishness—ridiculous bill, webbed feet—

the platypus seems to be a mammal.
So no platypus adorns the fake forest
of my living room. But now
I sort of regret it, and I've determined
to purchase a platypus
on my next visit south. Why?
1. Tourists have become native
to Bolivia, essential to her economy,
not to be disdained.
2. Great name, platypus. The fact
that I could not spell it
without Mr. Webster's help—and
had a hard time even locating
it—enhances its value.
3. Anything that, just by being itself,
makes me laugh deserves cherishing.
At this time of life, I need a platypus.

Gallivanting About

Gallivant is a lovely word.
Makes me think of Sir Gallahad
roaming the dales of Yorkshire,
riding through the heather
to slay dragons
and rescue damsels.

When I gallivant
no one composes
long poems about it. Never-
theless my feats
deserve mention
in at least a small poem.
So here it is.

Let it be known that...
    —once I rescued a blue-
    breasted hummingbird
    that flew into the kitchen
    window. I cupped its tiny
    body in my hands and prayed

hard. Eventually it stirred,
fluttered, and as I lifted it
into a tree, it levitated
and flew off.

—When I catch a spider
in the house, I always release
her into the garden.

—I love to wander on mountain
tops, but rarely do battle there.

—Even so, I have followed my
King into the deep wasted places
and at his bidding I have cast
invisible monsters into the pits
of hell.

If that isn't gallivanting,
nothing is.

3
The Absurdity of Prayer

Lord, have mercy on us all.

Close to the Ground

I choke on the word spirituality.
Not so much the reality
but the sometimes solitary focus
on the ethereal, mystical, and utterly
invisible. I lose my way in the mist.
My spirit hums closer
to the ground, often emerges
with mud on its face. It scrounges
truth among the mushrooms and
lichen. Peels off labels from
discarded tin cans, and there among
the roaches and other vagrants,
finds its theology in funky
configurations. Prefers single
syllable words and saints
with sullied reputations.
Loves it when Jesus plays
with little kids. Joins him
for hot dogs and Kool-Aid
afterwards. Laughs

during the prayer. Sometimes
forgets
to say "Amen."

Cheating at Sudoku

I'm a late-night Sudoku player,
and I cheat.
Especially at the end of the book
where the games are labeled
"challenger." When I get stuck
in the dark hours, I give myself
leeway so I can complete
what I began and go back to bed.
I record my lapses on a small
bald head, penciled in the margins.
I draw a single hair each time
I peek at the answers. Some heads
end up with only one hair,
some with three or five.
By the end of the game, if
I haven't peeked at all, I cover
the head with zeros, a curly,
triumphant crown. I draw
in a smile for wins, a frown
for losses. I figure this artistic
accountability makes me

an honest cheat.
It's like confession after sin.
In this case, I confess
to myself. I'm quick
to forgive.

North Valley Friends Church Discusses Human Sexuality

After the prerequisite silence
we move forward, "carefully
and without inappropriate pressure."
We seek a sense of the meeting
on matters of sensuality,
worshiping as we walk
through a mindfield of words.
Pacifists on tiptoe, we wonder
whether bonding comes before
procreation as the meaning
of marriage, decide it does.
Consensus on which distortions
to include eludes us. Should
we even mention distortions?
We try to map out "the journey
toward healing," define sexual
wholeness without the naming
of parts or positions.
After an hour-and-a-half we
have no unified statement but

we're all still friends. Maybe
that's enough. Maybe it's not.
Who says Quakers don't
speak in tongues?

Putting in the Pieces
(Friends "meeting for worship for business")

The meeting moved forward
slowly. The borders had been
established, and now different
ones were adding pieces,
filling in the middle of
this large puzzle.
An underwater scene was
emerging, an ocean that pulsed
with kelp, coral, fish, bubbles
and more light than was logical.
But large holes remained.
As I sat, one gnarly puzzle piece
swam through my brain, lodged
just behind my eyes. I couldn't
make sense of it at first, but all
at once I recognized a small
orange pair of fish lips.
"You've got to be kidding,"
I said to Spirit.
"Nope," she replied.
"But I can't offer this. It's silly."

"Yes, Nancy, you can." I felt
rather than saw her smile.
"Besides, if you don't put in
your piece, just think of that fish,
forever doomed to live
without its lips."
My giggle broke the surface
of the silence. When the quiet
again settled in,
I stood up.

Everyone's Right

I've decided that everyone's
right about everything.
And that if I listen carefully
to whoever's talking about
whatever subject, I just might hear
the part he's getting right.
The only thing is,
I can't speak.

When I'm alone again,
I remember the words, ideas and stories,
and I toss them high. I play. I
juggle. I watch the colors
sparkle in the sun. And when they
all fall down, I let them stay
where they land. Most end up
on the ground. The ones I catch
I throw up again and again until
I'm left with a singular
truth. I usually forget
where it came from.

The Elders Finally Do Something

They formed a committee.
The proper nouns invited
their improper sisters and brothers,
sat them down and explained,
in great detail, the Situation.
"This impropriety has simply,"
they said, "got to stop.
That's all there is to it."
And it was. After that
everything at church was good
again.

Deadheading the Irises

They've bloomed for us since May,
lifting their multicolored skirts
in a welcoming dance,
flinging rainbow colors
in greeting as members
of the local family of God,
also clad in varying colors,
styles and perspectives,
made their way past the garden
and into the sanctuary.

But the season is passing,
and Anna attends to the garden,
deadheading the early blooms
that now show signs of decay.
With scissors and a flick of her wrist,
she snaps them off.
Silverado, Rare Treat, Viva la France!,
Hello Darkness, Armageddon,
Dusky Challenger and *Mary Francis,*
painted ladies past their prime,

they all bite the dust as the few remaining
blossoms pretend it won't happen to them.

And even as I thank God for Anna's
service, tidying up the garden,
I recall that God's ways are above ours.
I think of those among us whose
sanctification occasionally slips,
give praise for a Master Gardener
who does not deadhead the saints.

A Reasonable Approach to War

If some worthy person in a far off country
is willing to die for his/her country and/or faith,
then the least I can do
is be willing to kill him/her
(for the sake of my country and/or faith).

To the Impatient Child

(a poem that is really a prayer)

Little one,
your time will come,
but not today.
Soon, you will come out
of hiding and greet
the world with a yell,
but not just yet.
Soon, you will meet
her face-to-face,
the one you only feel
now, blood-to-blood,
swimming in liquid love,
moving with her
in a dim, warm space.
Soon, you will meet
him, feel his heart
beat as he holds you
to his chest, pats
your back, hums,
but not now.

It's coming soon,
believe me—
real air on your face,
light, colors, music
and a whole open place
of people who will receive
you with so much love
you'll need time
to take it all in.
And time is what
we're asking for now.
So rest easy, settle back,
let yourself grow.
A world of wonders approaches.
But not today.

Moses and Me

Needing a clear word
from the Lord, I started
a fire in the vacant lot.
I struck a match and threw
it into a bush. The flame bud
blossomed into a fat,
red flower, spread and became
a field of wild flowers. Soon
the whole lot thrummed hotter
than bees and rose in waves
of its own making. Street
sirens accompanied
the performance.
God was nowhere to be heard.

Prayerless among the Branches

My imagination, unruly gift,
comes, I suppose, from God.
(I call her Agnes, to satisfy
my primal need to name the animals.)
She squirrels about in the maple tree
just outside my kitchen window,
flits from branch to branch,
only sits a few seconds to chomp
on some savory something,
then with a flounce, flies off again.
Sometimes she chases another squirrel
(let's call him Fred) who mysteriously
keeps hanging around, perpetual tease,
never letting himself be captured,
but not wandering too far away.
Why can't Agnes just sit quietly
in her lovely bower, feel the wind
ruffling her fur, give herself
over to prayer? In such a green and gracious
space, shouldn't prayer be natural?

Confession of a Failed Contemplative

Contemplative prayer is a lot like
snacking on sunflower seeds.
You just know something good
is waiting for you. That tangy taste
that teases the tongue tells you
a treat is in store if you only
keep probing. So you bite it in half,
suck the salt from the shells,
nibble the seed, small but savory,
then wonder if that's
all there is.

Meditation on Mark 4:35-41
Following an Oil Spill

I must have been seven years old
the first time I heard the story
of Jesus calming the storm.

Being young and credulous,
I accepted it simply. The fishermen's
amazement came to me

later in life. I, too, learned to question,
"Who then is this that even
the wind and the sea obey him?"

I also learned to question why
doesn't he do it now. I watch
on TV the oil creep up the shore

of south Florida, and I wonder
what the word of authority
would command and through

which channel the command

would flow. I guess I'm asking
how to pray to the One who is the same

yesterday today and forever. With what
words and to whom should I ask him to direct
them? To the ooze floating on the surface,

"Peace! Be dissolved!"?
To the breach on the ocean floor,
"Peace! Be closed!"?

Oh, Lord of the wind and the sea,
of the minerals and the gasses, of the fish
and the pelicans and the marshlands, say something

now. I strain to hear your voice
as the stench of our sin and the silence
of your people begin to overwhelm.

Lenten Poems from the Book of John

1. John 2:13-25

This harsh, angry Jesus alarms me.
He makes a weapon,
lifts it against both men and beasts.
He even attacks the furniture.
He throws money about
in what looks like a first class
temper tantrum, the seeds of war.
He yells and commands, casts
people out. Apparent pride
and a complete lack of trust
in his fellow human beings
round out this ugly portrait
of a man who scares me.
His Father may have
"so loved the world"
but his son doesn't appear
to even like it.

2. John 7:25-53

You need to work on your style,
Jesus. Have you noticed
that no one is laughing at
your jokes? If none of your
riddles have accessible answers
you'll soon lose your audience.
Your ratings have dropped.
Your future as a comedian
is in jeopardy. You need
to come up with something new.

3. John 11:38-57

Forgive me, Lord,
if the re-telling of this story
has made it so familiar
I lose the amazement.
I should gasp, scream,
cover my face, flee in fear.
Faint, at the very least.
Restore to me, my Lord,
the terror of resurrection.

4. John 15:1-17

How can I abide in you,
my Lord? I go for hours
without even thinking of you.
Prayerless days are not
uncommon, and if I'm
not in crisis mode, I find
my joy in other pursuits.
I don't naturally turn to you
in my open spaces. I don't
gravitate to the center.
Some kind of centrifugal
force spins me away,
in spite of my longing, my
very real longing, to abide.
Please help me. Pull me in
to you.

5. John 18:1-27

"I am he" is the seismic center.
It spreads in expanding rings.
The bodies fall outward,
circle a setting sun.
Torches, lanterns, weapons,
a bloody face, arrest
and betrayals spin,
but the center holds.

Even so, night deepens.
Even so, this unbearable cold.

6. John 18:28-40

"What is truth?"
the politician asks,
not sticking
around for an answer.
The question hangs
in the air while
the man born
to be king awaits
his coronation
in silence.

7. John 20:1-18

Missionary, apostle to the apostles,
beloved friend of Jesus,
tears still wet on your face,
it was love that thrust
you forth, joy that gave
your feet wings, wonder
that filled your voice
with gospel. Woman of God,
pure and trembling one,
you will remember always
his voice, "Mary," forever

calling your name, "Mary,"
causing you to run
from the garden to the city,
from Jerusalem to Bombay,
to Barcelona and Cleveland,
to Cochabamba and Kigali,
telling us all,
"I have seen the Lord!"

Some Unorthodox Commentary from the Book of James

At the Speed of Love

"Everyone should be quick to listen, slow to speak and slow to anger." (James 1:19)

Hurry! You can just about catch it
coming from behind
the barn—early morning insects,
dew dropping,
blades lifting. All of them
telling secrets.
****

Tiny quakers, a congress of mice,
their mouths stay shut,
but, oh!, how their whiskers quiver.
****

"You have two ears, only one mouth,"
the elders tell us, meaning, "Keep still."
I swallow the words, but they lump
in my stomach, refuse to dissolve.
I know my ears are scarlet.
I am far from perfection.

What Happens in the Dark

> "Humbly accept the word planted in you, which
> can save you." (James 1:21)

As I sit in the silence,
the seed deepens, puts down roots.
On the surface, nothing changes.
Not even a hint of the harvest
to come.

Unequal Match

> "Mercy triumphs over judgment." (James 2:13)

The crowd is going wild.
The contenders have marched in
and are seated in opposite corners.
Attendants hover around Judgment,
toweling his huge forehead,
massaging his biceps.
He sweats in anticipation, scowls
at his opponent, raises a victory
fist. Cheers reverberate,
pound the walls.
Mercy just sits there,
hands in her lap,
knowing what she knows.

Who? Me?

"Not many of you should presume to be teachers,
my brothers and sisters." (James 3:1)

You got that one right.
I shiver at the thought
of the men in my class—
leaders all of them, people
of prestige in their own circles.
The literature tells me I'm
not a teacher anyway. I'm
a facilitator, a guide, a fellow
learner, an along-side worker
in the construction of knowledge.
That's almost as ugly
as being called expert. The term
that fits me best is simply impostor.
Lord, have mercy on us all.

Dilemma

"Resist the devil and he will flee from you." (James 4:7)

The red suit, forked tail and horns
bit only appears in comic books.
The main problem with resisting
the devil is simply recognizing him
in the first place.

Not Safe

"Come near to God and God will come near to you."
(James 4:8)

After years of growing up in this house,
after all the warnings and hand slappings
—I am well trained, I am cautious—
why are you now telling me
to place my hand
on the glowing burner?

I'm no astronaut.
I barely made it through high school
physics. And you ask me
—without the suit, no oxygen tanks,
not even a rocket—to take a stroll
through the galaxies?

The Creator of volcanoes, black
holes, caterpillars and the beans
that morphed into this cup of coffee
has invited me over for a chat?
How do I get ready? What will
I wear? And whatever—in heaven
or on earth—will we talk about?

How does immaterial immensity
—or whatever God is—draw near
to an infinitesimal speck—that would
be me—without destroying it?

Where is the place big enough
for the meeting? Will it be an open field,
a mountain peak or a mansion?
How do I get there? A little girl again,
I dare to mumble my questions.

If I manage to find the place,
do I just ring the doorbell?
Will I be able to reach it?
Will a servant answer? Or God
himself? Do we shake hands?
What if he hasn't any?
How will I know it's really him?

Definitely not safe. An invitation
to play with fire, to enter
the ocean and swim with sharks,
to draw near to unbearable light.
Not safe. Not safe at all.

4
Longing for Home

*With a gentle but demanding attention to detail,
we prepare the soil. We plant. We wait.*

Preparing for Canonization

If someday, long after my death,
the church were to declare me a saint,
I want to be known as
Our Lady of Perpetual Astonishment.
Even now, I practice.
Consider
      —Lying in bed, I listen to the maple tree argue
      the wind, struggle to stay awake, don't want
      to miss any of it.
      —When I gather stones on the beach, I hear them
      sing in the palm of my hand.
      —I lick the salty tears from your face,
      savor your sorrow.
      —A walk in the woods; light swims through the firs,
      flips the shadows, shakes my bones.
Like Moses, I approach
the thick darkness where God is—
groping, breathless, ready.

Weary Roads

O rest beside the weary road, and hear the angels sing.
From "It Came Upon a Midnight Clear"

Do roads get tired?
Does the tramp of feet
and the turn of wheels
over the rough patina
of the streets cause
the weariness that comes
to all who lay down
their lives?

Wilson Road was not weary.
At least it didn't seem so
as I was growing up.
Its dirt surface welcomed
my pounding feet as nightly
my dog and I ran, while the stars
above poured down their dreams.

The Caranavi Road didn't dare
get weary or its collapse
would plunge us over the cliff
to the certain end of all dreams.

The Pan American Highway,
that section that crosses the Bolivian
altiplano, could possibly be called
a weary road, tired, I suppose,
of forcing its ruts and bumps
to live up to the hype of its name.

I remember an unnamed road
that snaked across the altiplano,
roughly following the contours
of the land. It eventually bogged down
in a river. Beyond weary,
it simply lay down and died.

The Hollywood Freeway vibrated
with so much tension that sooner
or later weariness was inevitable.

The Wilson River Road winds up
through the pines on its way to the sea.
Ever perky, never tired. It knows
what's ahead.

On all these roads, weary or not,
the angels sang. I hear them now.

Pure Joy

> "Consider it pure joy, my brothers and sisters, whenever you face trials of many kinds." (James 1:2)

It starts out low and slowly builds,
a groundswell of holy laughter.
It mushrooms from forest
floors. Out of the darkness a thread
of light floats, begins to weave.
—*Oui, sí, ya, jisa jisa*—
From around the world, people
are saying *Yes!* They get it.
In hospital rooms, at the scene
of the crime, from refugee camps,
even at grave sites it comes—
the improbable chuckle,
the inappropriate snort, a giggle
in the night. Dag Hammarkskjold
once wrote, —For all that has been,
thanks. For all that will be, yes.—
It's not faith but mirth
that moves these mountains.

Secret Sowers

"Peacemakers who sow in peace raise a harvest of
righteousness." (James 3:18)

We lay down our seeds in the dark.
Spring has been exceptionally cold
this year. Reluctant daffodils
have done little to convince me.
But we do the work of the faithful
farmer, rising in the predawn hours.
It is a chosen hiddenness, a subtle
stretching over time, ear bent to listen
to the ground, ready for instruction.
Slow, rhythmic movements are best.
Sometimes we simply show up,
holding borrowed pain, applying tears
or not. With a gentle but demanding attention
to detail, we prepare the soil.
We plant. We wait.

Improvisations

> "The practice of resurrection encourages improvisation
> on the basic resurrection story." —Eugene Peterson

The day Grandma died
something quickened in the atmosphere.
A breeze sashayed
through the cherry orchard.
Unseen stars kicked up their heels
in the day-blind sky.

****

Cancer ward. My friend Sandi
fights nausea. Hope hides
its bright face but refuses
to disappear altogether.
Outside in the evening
pond frogs croak,
"Kyrie eleison.
Kyrie eleison."

****

Peter turns seven.
At his request we go to Red Robin
for hamburgers. As the waiters
gather at a neighboring table
to sing a loud and public "Happy Birthday,"
Peter leans in and announces,
"They're going to do that to me next."
And they do.

****

On my early morning walk,
hundreds of calendar-defying daffodils
greet me, all of them grinning
like stewardesses.

****

Dwaine's death stuns. My friend
and colleague, a husband, father,
grandfather. Running on the beach.
Not old. Not old at all. It's like
those something-is-wrong-
with-this-picture puzzles I did
as a child. Lord, help us trace our way
through the shadowed places. Splash
in some resurrection hues.

All Things

"For from him and through him and to him are all things.
To him be the glory forever. Amen." (Romans 11:36)

All things.

Clods, clumps, bunches and sorts.

All of it. Nothing is to be left out, ignored or named
insignificant.

Every lump. Inside the circle.

And the circle spins slowly

spins out from the heart of the Christ

twirls in and through and down the channels of light

and comes back to its lovely genesis

from him
and
through him
and
to him.

All things.

Solid things
rocks, the mountain (my mountain)

outside my childhood home in Ramona,
my copy of *War and Peace*, this coffee mug,
the Turkish rug at my feet.

Gaseous things
    steam from my coffee, the sun,
    morning mist off the river, principalities and powers,
    oxygen, the Holy Ghost.

Things that stay
    some promises, the sky, the praises of God's people.

Things that once seemed solid but disappeared when poked
    my parents, the house I grew up in, the ice plant
    in front, my dog, my trophy for best actress,
    my place in line.

Things they tell me are real and I take by faith (or try to)
    molecules, democracy, best friends,
    peace on earth good will to men (and women),
    germs, antibodies, love.

Things I take pleasure in
    the purple orchids in the tangerine tree, cicada song
    in spring, my body, Vivaldi, pan pipes, cold water
    on a hot day, the early morning of any day, grand-
        children.

Things that frighten me
> the mortality of my loved ones, my best friend's stroke,
> teaching, large groups of people all talking at once or
> > taking turns
> and soon it will be me, snakes.

Little things
> dew drops, short words (salt, sand, toad, fuzz),
> one minute prayers, eight minute eggs, my husband's
> smile, a hand on the shoulder.

Gigantic things
> the ocean (standing on a mountain in Oregon, looking
> > west),
> floods in Haiti, refugee camps, the Universal Church,
> the night sky at Samaipata, the Bolivian altiplano,
> the Andes.

Problematic things
> my job at the university, Camba culture, road blocks
> and hunger strikes, making money, being Anglo-Saxon
> in a Latin country, being a human resource.

Hopeful things
> "Christ in me the hope of glory," heaven, peace on earth
> good will to women (men too), a mature and gently
> > lovely
> old age.

All things tangible, intangible
All goals, drives, dreams and dreads
All tears and sighs
All joy.

All lights and loves, favorite old poems and those to be
    written
gall stones, fairy tales and the river that joins them.

Everywhere and everywhen
Everywho and everyhow.

All things

    from, through, to him

    Glory.

Acknowledgments

Thanks to the following publications in which some of the poems in this book first appeared:

At the Speed of Love: A Small Collection of Poems: "Mother Tongue," "God's Tiny Hand," "The Poet's Gifts," "I'm Sorry," "At the Speed of Love," "Prayerless among the Branches," "Weary Roads," "Who? Me?"

Peace with Justice (a Northwest Yearly Meeting blog): "A Reasonable Approach to War"

Poems of Peace: "Secret Sower"

Truth's Bright Embrace: Essays and Poems in Honor of Arthur O. Roberts: "I Love a Tangent"

CPSIA information can be obtained
at www.ICGtesting.com
Printed in the USA
FSOW01n0247160417
33051FS

9 781594 980367